Juan Gonzalez

OUTSTANDING OUTFIELDER

BY BILL GUTMAN

MILLBROOK SPORTS WORLD
THE MILLBROOK PRESS
BROOKFIELD, CONNECTICUT

Photographs courtesy of Focus on Sports: cover, cover inset, pp. 4, 8, 10, 11, 12, 14 (left), 26, 39, 40-41, 46; AP/Wide World: pp. 3, 29, 32; *The Dallas Morning News*: pp. 6 (Louis DeLuca), 22 (Cindy Yamanaka); Allsport: pp. 14 (right, Jonathan Daniel), 17 (Jonathan Daniel), 21 (J. Patronite), 25 (Jed Jacobsohn), 30 (Jonathan Daniel), 34 (Jonathan Daniel), 20 (Otto Greule), 42 (Jonathan Daniel), 44 (Otto Greule); Copyright 1990, Oklahoma Publishing Company. From the August 29, 1990 issue of *The Daily Oklahoman*: p. 19.

Library of Congress Cataloging-in-Publication Data
Gutman, Bill
Juan Gonzales, outstanding outfielder / by Bill Gutman
p. cm. — (Millbrook sports world)
A biography of baseball star outfielder Juan Gonzalez, from his childhood in Puerto Rico to his success with the Texas Rangers to his dedication to the youth of Puerto Rico.
ISBN 1-56294-567-X
1. Gonzalez, Juan, 1969—Juvenile literature. 2. Baseball players—Puerto Rico—Biography—Juvenile literature.
I. Title. II. Series.
GV865.G61G88   1995
796.357′092—dc20   [B]   94-48161   CIP   AC

Published by The Millbrook Press, Inc.
2 Old New Milford Road
Brookfield, Connecticut 06804

JUAN GONZALEZ

It was Sunday, October 4—the last day of the 1992 baseball season. The Texas Rangers were playing their final game. The team was in fourth place in the American League's Western Division. They were in the midst of another losing season. So the final game against the California Angels at Anaheim, California, meant very little.

There was one player on the Rangers, however, to whom the game meant a great deal. Juan Gonzalez, the 22-year-old Texas outfielder, was trying to put a cap on his second full major league season. It had been quite a year for him. Going into his team's final game, Juan was tied with Oakland's Mark McGwire for the American League home run crown, with 42.

It was with a mighty swing like this that Juan Gonzalez slammed his 43rd home run on the final day of the 1992 season to finish as the best home run hitter in the American League.

The power behind the hitter: Gonzalez drives the ball into the outfield.

Winning the home run title meant a lot to Juan. But, like most ballplayers, he would rather have his team win a championship. Since that wasn't going to happen in 1992, hitting the most home runs in the American League as well as in the majors was important.

So the 6-foot-3 (191-centimeter), 210-pound (141-kilogram) slugger came to bat with a purpose. With his powerful shoulders and muscular arms, he looked every bit like a power hitter. Standing on the right side of the plate, he concentrated on each pitch. Facing veteran right-hander Bert Blyleven, Juan finally got one that he liked and sent a rocket into the left field seats. Home run number 43.

Juan's homer broke the tie with McGwire, helped his team to a 9–5 victory, and gave him the home run crown. Within hours of the game's end he had cleaned out his locker and made plans to return home. The next day his plane landed at the airport in San Juan, Puerto Rico. There were 5,000 fans there to greet him. In his native Puerto Rico, Juan Gonzalez was quickly becoming a hero.

At the airport, a motorcade was set up to take him the 23 miles (37 kilometers) to his home in Vega Baja. There were 15 police officers on motorcycles escorting him through the streets. It was estimated that 100,000 people lined the Baldorioty Expressway to cheer and honor Juan. Another 3,000 people gathered in the main plaza of Vega Baja. They, too, were there to see Juan Gonzalez.

The entire experience was very moving to him. He had won a home run championship in America. But his baseball skills were making him a hero in his native land. That's what was important. He wanted to act in a responsible way, and he wanted to give something back to his people. When asked about his reaction to all the people who came to see him, this big, strong man said, "I remember that I cried."

GROWING UP IN ALTO DE CUBA

The Commonwealth of Puerto Rico is an island located just east of Cuba and the Dominican Republic. It has the Caribbean Sea to the south and the Atlantic Ocean to the north. It is a self-governing part of the United States and is

represented in the United States Congress by a resident commissioner who has a voice, but no vote.

Although the island has a mostly Latino culture, Puerto Ricans are citizens of the United States. There are more than 3.5 million living on the island, which was discovered by Columbus in 1493. Puerto Rico was first settled by the Spanish in 1508. It was ceded, or surrendered, to the United States after the Spanish-American War (1898). In 1952 the people of the island voted to make Puerto Rico a commonwealth.

There have been many famous people from Puerto Rico, including artists, scientists, musicians, doctors, actors, and sports stars. Baseball has always been a huge sport in Puerto Rico, and some of the great Puerto Rican big leaguers include Roberto Clemente, Tony Perez, and Orlando Cepeda.

So there was a legacy for Juan Gonzalez to follow. He was born in the city of Vega Baja on October 16, 1969. His father, also named Juan, was a math teacher in Vega Baja for some thirty years. His mother, Lele, raised her children and spent some time working in a General Electric factory.

The oldest child in the family was named Juan, as well. He was ten years older than young Juan. There were also two sisters, Blanquita and Lindi. The family lived in a district of Vega Baja called Alto de Cuba.

As young Juan grew up, Alto de Cuba was becoming more dangerous. There was more and more poverty in the district during those years, and with poverty came drugs. Many of the young boys began to find themselves pulled into that dark world of drugs, violence, and crime. Meanwhile, young Juan began to discover something else—baseball.

Juan's parents, Juan and Lele
Gonzalez, at their home in Puerto Rico.

When he was a boy in Puerto Rico, Juan spent a great deal of time at a neighborhood bodega (grocery store). Whenever he returns home, one of the first people Juan visits is the owner, El Chino, pictured here with Juan at the store.

A man named El Chino, who ran a bodega, or grocery store, in Cuba de Alto, remembers Juan coming into his shop to buy some candy. Juan and his friends would be barefoot, but always ready to play ball. They used a broomstick for a bat and a bottle cap for a ball.

When Juan was 10, he was a big fan of professional wrestling. His favorite wrestler at the time was named "The Mighty Igor." Juan liked him so much that his friends soon began calling him "Igor." The name stuck. Nicknames made things easier around the Gonzalez house, since all three males were named Juan. His father and older brother already had nicknames: His father was called Chon, his brother Puma.

About that same time the barrio, or district, of Alta de Cuba was deteriorating rapidly. Puma was running with the wrong crowd and slowly becoming involved with drugs. It would become a bigger problem as the years passed. A good friend of Juan's, Luis Mayoral, says that when Juan was about 10 he had already made a decision never to become involved with drugs. Young Juan seemed to understand what was happening to his brother.

The Alto de Cuba section of Vega Baja became a very dangerous place to live when Juan was a boy. Yet he returns there often now, where he tries to help youngsters find the right road in life.

The great Roberto Clemente was not only a Hall of Fame ballplayer, but a hero in Puerto Rico as well. Early in his life, Juan Gonzalez wanted to follow in Clemente's footsteps.

"It was as a if a little red light suddenly came on," Mayoral, who now works for the Rangers as a public relations liaison to the Latino community, said.

Juan's parents also knew about the dangers of Alto de Cuba, and they began looking to get out. Finally, when Juan was 13, the family was able to move across Highway 2 and into a safer community. While Juan would always stay out of trouble, he would never forget Alto de Cuba and the lessons he learned there. Unlike many others who left Alto de Cuba and found success later in life, Juan Gonzalez would make it a point to return.

THE MAKING OF A BALLPLAYER

Once the family had moved, Juan began getting more and more involved in baseball. He already knew about some of the other fine players who had come out of Puerto Rico. As did other youngsters, the player he knew the most about was Roberto Clemente. Everyone in Puerto Rico knew about him.

Clemente played for the Pittsburgh Pirates for 18 seasons and was one of the finest all-around ballplayers in baseball history. But he was more than a great baseball player. He was also a special person, who worked very hard to help the poor people of Puerto Rico and other Latin countries.

Then, suddenly, on December 31, 1972, Roberto Clemente was killed in a plane crash while he was taking food and supplies to Managua, Nicaragua, a city that had been hit by a huge earthquake.

His last dream was realized after he died. The Roberto Clemente Sports City is a place where kids can learn about sports and about being good citizens as well. That was what Clemente had always wanted.

Juan Gonzalez heard about Clemente early. He knew he was a great player, but he also knew about the other things Clemente did. This legacy would play a large part in Juan Gonzalez's later life.

But first he had to work on becoming a ballplayer. Juan started playing in Little League, then moved to the Babe Ruth League. He played constantly as he grew bigger and stronger.

When Juan was about 15 he joined the American Legion baseball program. His parents worked very hard and didn't see him play often. Then one night there was a knock at the door. When his father answered it, he found Juan standing there with his baseball coach.

"What are you feeding this kid?" the coach asked.

At first, Juan Sr. didn't know what to think. He asked the coach why he wanted to know. Then the coach smiled.

"Because your son hit three huge home runs today," the coach said. "It was one of the most incredible things I've seen in a long time."

Juan's father remembered that as a turning point. "It was the first time I realized that Juan really had something special."

After that, things began moving very quickly. Major league scouts are always looking at players from Puerto Rico and other Latin American countries. So it was no surprise that just a year later a scout for the Texas Rangers arrived at the Gonzalez home.

Juan was already over 6 feet (183 centimeters) tall and weighed 170 pounds (114 kilograms). He was just 16 years old but had become a very strong player and powerful hitter. The scout's name was Luis Rosa. He explained that the Rangers were prepared to offer Juan a professional baseball contract with a bonus of $75,000.

Young Juan couldn't believe his ears. He and his parents went into the kitchen for a family meeting. They returned a few minutes later, and Juan Sr. signed the contract for his son.

The date was May 30, 1986.

"After I signed Juan," Luis Rosa recalled, "I told a TV station that I just signed the top young home run hitter to come out of Latin America."

That summer, Juan packed his bags and left home for the first time. The Rangers told him to report to Sarasota in Florida, to play in the rookie Gulf Coast League. That was the first stop in the minors.

Juan was one of the youngest players on the team. But he impressed Rangers' then assistant general manager Sandy Johnson, who remembered the first time he saw him.

"He was only 16 and a gangly kid," Johnson said. "But he had a big frame, and you could tell he was a good athlete. He had tremendous bat speed,

Juan developed his batting style early and kept it through the minors and into the majors. It is very similar to that of his idol, Roberto Clemente (left).

long arms, and a natural power hitter's swing. We felt right from the beginning we had something special."

But no matter how good he might look, a 16-year-old is not ready for the
big leagues. And no young player is ever a sure thing. In fact, at Sarasota
Juan played well but didn't show any real signs of becoming a leading power
hitter. He was in 60 games, getting 56 hits in 233 at bats for a less than great
.240 batting average. Surprisingly, 51 of those hits were singles. He had 4
doubles, 1 triple, but not one home run.

As soon as the year ended, Juan returned home and to high school. He
worked hard to graduate with his class in 1987. Then the Rangers told
him to report to Gastonia in the South Atlantic League. He was ready to make
his push toward the major leagues.

GROWING TIME

At Class A Gastonia, Juan became a real ballplayer. He played every day and
began hitting with power. This was more like it. At mid-season he played in
the league all-star game, then finished strong.

In 1987, Juan hit .265 with 21 doubles, 2 triples, 14 home runs, and 74
runs batted in (RBI). He wasn't great defensively, but was working hard at it.
In addition, he swiped 9 bases in 13 tries.

"Juan had the kind of work ethic that impressed everyone in the organi-
zation," said a Rangers scout who kept tabs on the minor leagues. "All his
skills improved in 1987, and he was showing signs of becoming an outstanding power hitter. Everyone still felt he was the real goods."

From Gastonia, Juan moved up to Charlotte in 1988. Charlotte was another Class A team that played in the Florida State League. Only this time

there was a slight setback: On April 20, just after the season started, Juan suffered a knee injury.

He had to undergo arthroscopic surgery and missed nearly two months of the season. He wound up playing in just 77 games, hitting .256 with 8 homers and 43 RBI. Still, the Rangers saw progress. In 1989, Juan was again brought to the next level. He was assigned to the Tulsa Drillers, a Class AA team in the Texas League.

It turned out to be an all-star year for Juan. He batted .293 in 133 games, belting out 21 homers and driving in 85 runs. He also had 30 doubles and 7 triples. He was among the league leaders in almost all offensive categories and was now considered a true power hitter.

Then, on September 1, he got his first call to the majors. At that point in the season, big league teams can bring up some of the top minor leaguers. The Rangers were anxious to take a look at their 19-year-old slugger.

Juan started 19 of the team's final 31 games and pinch-hit in 5 others. He played mostly in center field, which wasn't his

Juan got his first taste of the majors at the end of the 1989 season. This is one of his first games in a Texas uniform. He already looks good at the plate.

natural position, and he seemed a bit overmatched at the plate. He hit just .150 with 9 hits in 60 at bats. But he belted his first big league homer and finished with 7 RBI. Asked if he was nervous being in the big leagues, Juan answered quickly. "No," he said. "Only one time, in the first game."

But that didn't mean Juan was in the majors to stay. He returned home in the off-season and played winter ball at Caguas in the Puerto Rican League. Playing back in Puerto Rico was something he enjoyed. The kids were getting to know him, and he talked with them all the time.

Even then, Juan felt that he would soon have a role in helping the children of his native land. That was one of the reasons he worked so hard at baseball. He knew that if he became a star in the big leagues, people would look up to him. Then it would be easier to help.

"I always had this feeling that something big was going to happen to me," he once said. "God gives me certain flashes. It's hard to describe. It's something natural. It's like a joy that I feel."

So he looked forward to the 1990 season as perhaps his final step to the majors. This time the Rangers sent him to Class AAA Oklahoma City in the American Association. Juan had gone from Class A to AA and now to AAA. His play had improved at each level.

At age 20, he was the youngest player in the American Association, but he didn't play like it. In fact, the 1990 season turned out to be Juan's breakout year. It was the year he convinced everybody that he was a rising star.

Playing for AAA Oklahoma City in 1990, Juan became the Most Valuable Player in the American Association and the Rangers Minor League Player of the Year. He walloped 29 homers and showed he was ready for the big leagues.

"From the opening week of the season, it was apparent to everyone that Juan was the best player in the league," said one writer who covered the American Association. "He was playing with the kind of confidence you rarely see in a 20-year-old. You could see that he was just a step away from the big leagues."

BIG LEAGUER

Juan played well for the entire American Association season. He wound up leading the league with 29 homers, 101 RBI, and 252 total bases. The only negative was a mediocre .258 batting average. But the Rangers figured that would change with experience. After the season he was named the league's Most Valuable Player as well as Rookie of the Year. The Rangers also named him their Minor League Player of the Year.

On August 29 of that year the Rangers once again called him to Arlington, Texas, to join the parent club. He was in the majors for the second straight September.

This time the Rangers wanted a better look. The team was out of the race by September and were already looking to 1991. Juan started 14 games in the outfield and 8 more as the designated hitter. When Juan failed to get a single hit in his first 11 at bats, Rangers manager Bobby Valentine and everyone else was worried. Would Juan start to feel intimidated by big league pitching?

Juan told everyone he wasn't nervous and wasn't worried. Then he began to hit. During one 10-game stretch in September, he hit 4 home runs. In fact, after his 0-for-11 start, he bore down and hit .329 the rest of the way. That gave him a total batting average of .289 in 25 games. He had 26 hits in 90 at bats, including 7 doubles, 4 homers, and 12 runs batted in.

The Rangers had seen enough. They decided that Juan Gonzalez would be a big part of their team in 1991.

The Rangers were a ball club that had always had a tough time winning. The team started as an expansion franchise in Washington, D.C., in 1961 and had 11 straight losing seasons before moving to Texas prior to the 1972 campaign.

In Texas, the team continued to struggle. Although it did manage a few winning seasons and a couple of second-place finishes, for the most part the ball club was disappointing. But there was new hope in 1991.

The Rangers had a hard-hitting team that year, led by Puerto Rican-born Ruben Sierra. First baseman Rafael Palmeiro and second sacker Julio Franco could also hit with power. It was hoped that Juan would fit right in and give Texas yet another big bat. The team worried more about their pitching than their hitting.

Juan had a temporary setback during spring training. He tore cartilage in his right knee and had arthroscopic surgery on

When he joined the Rangers for the 1991 season, Juan played alongside Ruben Sierra (21), another Puerto Rican–born star. Here the two chat before the start of an early season game.

Hitting wasn't the only thing Juan showed the rest of the American League in 1991. He proved he could play the outfield too. Here he races to the wall to make a fine running catch just behind the outstretched glove of center fielder Gary Pettis (24).

March 21. He missed the rest of spring training and then the first 12 games of the regular season. On April 26 he was finally activated. And he began hitting almost immediately.

Up to that point the team had not been playing well. Then between May 9 and 11, the Rangers lost three straight to Boston. The next day, they began a winning streak that would reach 13 games. And Juan Gonzalez became a major part of that streak. He was hitting for both power and average.

In the 13th game of the streak, the Rangers and Seattle Mariners were tied in the 11th inning. Juan came up and belted a two-run homer as part of a Texas rally to help his team to still another victory. In fact, many observers felt the turnaround of the Rangers began when Juan came off the disabled list. In a *Sports Illustrated* magazine story on the Rangers, writer Tim Kurkjian said that once off the disabled list, Juan "began establishing himself as the best young player in the league."

Texas third-base coach Dave Oliver said that many people around the league were asking about Juan. "People ask me how good he's been," Oliver said. "I don't even want to tell them. That's how good."

Juan was hitting at .343 after the 13th win of the streak and had already driven home 30 runs. By the All-Star break he was still hitting a solid .303. After that, both Juan and the team slowed their pace.

The longer season in the majors increases the pressure on the players, and maybe Juan was getting tired. But he was still hitting enough to impress people. Unfortunately, the Rangers were fading. By the second week of August they trailed not only the Minnesota Twins but the Chicago White Sox and Oakland A's as well.

In early August, however, there was a poll taken among the major league general managers. They wanted to know which young player in the majors was considered the best building block for a franchise.

Most of the answers were predictable. Some of the names that appeared were Ken Griffey, Jr., Barry Bonds, Kirby Puckett, and Barry Larkin. All had been in the league a few years already. But one general manager surprised everyone when he voted for Juan Gonzalez. Juan had been in the majors only four months, and here was a veteran baseball man who was ready to build a team around him.

"He looks like he's made the adjustments in his first year and will only get better," said the general manager who voted for Juan. "He's hitting the breaking ball the second time around. He has power, he'll start stealing bases, and his defense will only get better. He'll be like [teammate Ruben] Sierra, only better."

Even though the Rangers finished in the middle of the pack, Juan Gonzalez had a fine first season. He wound up with a .264 average in 142 games. But he also had 34 doubles, 27 home runs, and 102 runs batted in. The only downside was that he hit just .233 after the All-Star break. He was going to have to be more consistent. Still, there was little doubt that he was looked upon as one of the finer young players in the majors.

HOME RUN KING

In 1992, Juan was already considered a big part of the Rangers team. Once again the ball club appeared to have some really heavy hitters. Franco was injured, but young third sacker Dean Palmer looked like another bona fide power hitter. Sierra and Palmeiro were back, and a young catcher named Ivan "Pudge" Rodriguez, was also thought to be a coming star.

Once again the big problem was pitching. There weren't enough quality starters and no top bullpen closer. Despite the solid hitting, it was apparent that the club would have a struggle just to reach .500 in 1992.

Juan was forced to play center field for a good part of the year, even though he didn't have the blazing speed to be a top-notch center fielder. But he was hitting with more power than ever before.

One reason was Juan's conditioning program. He lifted weights during the off-season and was stronger than ever. His weight was up to a muscular 210 pounds (141 kilograms). Batting from the right side of the plate, he would lift his left leg high in the air as he stepped into a pitch.

The homers began coming more often. On June 7, against the Minnesota Twins, he blasted three long shots out of the park. But during a good part of the year he struggled to keep his batting average around the .250 mark.

His power numbers, however, were as good as any player's in the majors, and he was still just 22 years old. The only bad part was that the Rangers were again a struggling ball club. Then, on August 31, the team made a major trade. They sent Ruben Sierra and pitchers Jeff Russell and Bobby Witt to the Oakland A's in exchange for slugger Jose Canseco.

Canseco was a monster power hitter when healthy. The team hoped that in the upcoming years, Canseco and Gonzalez would become the most feared slugging duo in the league.

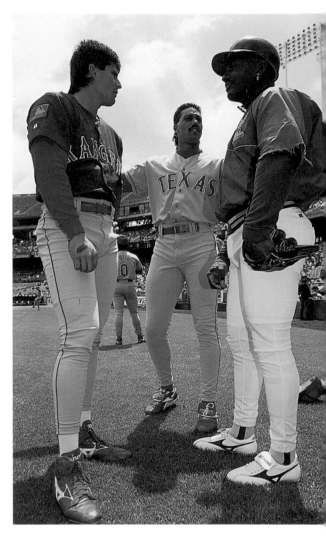

In August 1992, the Rangers traded Ruben Sierra and two pitchers to Oakland in return for slugger Jose Canseco. The team hoped Canseco and Juan would become a great slugging tandem. Here Canseco (left) and Juan, visit with Sierra (right) after the trade.

Juan never stops working. Part of his routine includes weight training. His muscular arms and shoulders help him hit his long home runs.

The team checked in with a 77–85 record and a fourth-place finish in the division. But it was Juan who made the biggest news. This was the year that he cracked his 43rd home run on the final day of the season to win the league crown. That also gave him the most homers of anyone in the majors.

Along with his 43 round-trippers, Juan also had a career best 109 runs batted in and a .260 batting average. Overall, it had been an outstanding season. Yet almost all of his teammates felt he was just scratching the surface.

"He's the kind of guy who you'll look back on and say, 'It was an honor playing with him,'" said Dean Palmer, who hit 26 homers himself. "I'm talking about Hall of Fame caliber. He's that special."

Juan had indeed opened some eyes. He became the fifth-youngest home run leader in baseball history. Only four other players in history had hit 40 home runs at a younger age. They were Mel Ott, Joe DiMaggio, Eddie Mathews, and Johnny Bench—all Hall of Fame greats. He was the first Texas Ranger and only the second Puerto Rican–born player to win a home run title. That also made Juan proud.

"I want to be an example for Puerto Rico," he said. "I am proud of the attention I have brought to my hometown. My priority is the youth. We as adults must work day by day and hand in hand for a better future for our youth."

Then came 1993. The Rangers had high hopes. This year they would have Jose Canseco from day one. There was also Palmer, Palmeiro, Rodriguez, and Franco. But before it ended, all of them would be overshadowed by Juan Gonzalez. This was the year he would step to the head of the class.

Playing only in left field and batting cleanup, Juan was having a career season. Not only was he hitting homers and driving in runs, but his batting average was up around the .300 mark. He was striking out less and making contact more. And he was having some big days.

The first came on June 8, when he slammed a huge home run at home against Minnesota. The blast measured 448 feet (137 meters) and was the longest home run ever hit in Arlington Stadium.

Then in a game against the California Angels on June 17, he produced the best day of his career. Early in the game, he stepped up and slammed a three-run homer. When he came up again the bases were loaded, and Ken

Patterson was on the mound. Juan got a pitch he liked, kicked that front leg up and whacked the ball deep into the left field seats for a grand slam. He circled the bases with a big smile on his face.

Later in the same game he rapped an RBI single. That gave him 8 runs batted in on the day. Now he was not only being called one of the best *young* players in the game, but one of the best players, period.

Although the team had a winning record under new manager Kevin Kennedy, there was one setback. Jose Canseco injured his elbow and needed surgery. After just 231 at bats and 10 homers, he was finished for the season. Now there was even more pressure on Juan to produce big numbers.

In July he was selected to the American League All-Star team for the first time. The day before the game there was a home run–hitting contest between the top sluggers in each league. It was Juan who came out on top. One of his shots became the first ball ever hit into the third deck in left field at the Baltimore Orioles' new ballpark at Camden Yards.

"This kid is a powerhouse," said a National League coach who had never seen Juan play before. "We heard that he was good, but one look at him and you can see he has the talent to be one of the best."

The only rap on Juan in 1993 was that he was somewhat streaky. He would be red hot for a couple of weeks, then suddenly go ice cold at the plate. But he was hot more often than not. By August 5, he was hitting at an impressive .336 clip for the year.

A proud and happy Juan shows off the trophy he received for winning the home run-hitting contest prior to the 1993 All-Star Game at Baltimore. One of his shots was the first ball ever hit into the third deck at the Orioles new park, Camden Yards.

JUSTICE 02
PIAZZA 00
BONDS 05
THE 1993 GATO
HOME RUN D
CHAMPION
JUAN GONZALEZ 12
AMERICAN 21
LEGG MASON
SONY

"I can see Juan winning the triple crown one of these years," said one of his teammates. "If he keeps getting better he's going to be downright scary."

Juan's play was a big reason the Rangers finally had a winning season at 86–76. They finished in second place, eight games behind the Chicago White Sox in the American League West.

Juan led the Rangers with a .310 batting average, 46 home runs, and 118 runs batted in. His 46 round-trippers topped the American League for the second straight year and tied him with Barry Bonds for the major league lead. He was twelfth in hitting, finished fourth in RBI, and first in homers. And he would have done even better had he not missed 22 games due to injuries.

That wasn't all. After the season he made every American League All-Star team and finished fourth in the Most Valuable Player balloting. He was also one of the three outfielders on the Major League All-Star team and won the Buck Canel Award as Latin American Player of the Year. That last award made him especially proud.

There were other milestones in his still-young career. Eleven of his home runs won games for the Rangers. He was also only the sixth player in history to hit as many as 46 homers in a season before his 24th birthday. And his 116 home runs over the previous three seasons set a record in the majors during that time.

This was a familiar sight to Rangers fans during the 1993 season. Juan saw the ball so well that he powdered 46 home runs to lead the American League as part of a great all-around season that saw him named to the Major League All-Star team.

His defense had also improved. He made just one error in his first 60 games and four all year.

"Juan worked very hard on his defense," said Luis Mayoral, his friend and a Rangers publicist. "He was 100 percent better defensively in 1993. Juan takes great pride in his defense and has become one of the best left fielders in the league."

It had taken only three full years in the majors for Juan Gonzalez to become a superstar.

OVERCOMING OBSTACLES

Prior to the start of the 1994 season, Juan was rewarded by the Rangers for his outstanding play. He was given a huge, long-term contract extension through the 1998 season with options for the two years after that. The contract, with the options, was worth an incredible $45 million. Juan was now among the highest paid athletes in all of sports.

But he had little time to celebrate. Shortly after the season started, tragedy struck the Gonzalez family. His older brother Puma died as a result of his longtime drug abuse.

"Puma had been in deep trouble for many years," said Luis Mayoral. "Like the rest of his family, Juan was devastated by the tragedy. But he managed to turn his brother's death into a positive. It just made him more resolved than ever to work with kids and try to keep them away from drugs."

A happy Juan Gonzalez speaks to the media after signing
a huge contract extension in February 1994. He became
one of the highest paid players in all of baseball.

Juan knew he had to return to the team as quickly as possible. The season promised to be an interesting one. Each league had been broken up into three divisions instead of two. The new American League West consisted of the Rangers, the Oakland A's, Seattle Mariners, and California Angels. It was predicted to be the weakest division in the league.

The Rangers were early favorites to win the West. Canseco was healthy again. First baseman Will Clark, who had been a big star with San Francisco, joined the team as a free agent. Palmeiro and Franco left via the same route. The problem again was the pitching.

Two things became evident early on. One was that all four teams in the division had weaknesses. None of them was playing .500 ball. While the Rangers had the lead during the first months of the season, it was still a struggle. And the other thing that became evident was that Juan Gonzalez was struggling as well.

By May 1, he was hitting in the .230 range with just 3 homers and 13 RBI. "I need to be more relaxed at the plate," Juan said. "I'm tight. I'm putting more pressure on myself with men on base. I need to be more patient. This is the first time in my career that I've started this slowly. I think that because of my big contract that sometimes I try too hard."

Fortunately, both Clark and Canseco were hitting well, with Jose really bashing the ball. Clark was hitting third and Canseco fourth. Juan was dropped to fifth in the lineup. It was a tougher slot to hit from. Pitchers often worked around the fifth-place hitter because the sixth hitter wasn't as strong. Still, Juan felt his game would fall into place.

Hard work has made Juan a fine outfielder as well as a top slugger. Here he lobs the ball back to the infield after making a fine running catch.

"Rafael Palmeiro struggled in April last year and look at the season he had," Juan said. "Barry Bonds is starting slowly this year."

Manager Kevin Kennedy felt that Juan had to focus more and be more selective. He was swinging at too many bad pitches.

"A lot of things are coming at Juan," the manager said. "He has a new contract and expects more of himself, and he's getting over the death of his brother. He just needs to get in focus at the plate. He needs to take more balls. Until he starts walking he won't get a lot of good pitches."

By the All-Star break Juan was starting to hit the ball better. The Rangers continued to lead the division with a sub-.500 record. Then something else hit the news. The baseball players union and the owners could not agree on a new contract. The players threatened a strike, or work stoppage, sometime in August if no agreement was reached.

It was a year in which some of the other young power hitters in the league were putting up big numbers. Ken Griffey, Jr., Frank Thomas, and Albert Belle were all having outstanding seasons. That meant Juan had to take a backseat in the headlines. Then, just when he was beginning to look like the old Juan Gonzalez, the players decided to strike.

Baseball stopped on August 12, as the two sides began meeting to see if they could resolve the crisis. The Rangers had a 52–62 record at the time of the strike. They led the division by one game over Oakland and two over Seattle.

After a slow start in 1994, Juan really began to powder the baseball. Here he blasts another long home run just days before the players' strike on August 12 that ended the baseball season. The tremendous power in his swing is very apparent.

At the time of the strike, Juan had his batting average up to a season high of .275. He had 19 home runs and 85 runs batted in. So he was certainly headed for his fourth consecutive 100 RBI season. And he looked as if he was ready to resume his position as one of baseball's best young sluggers.

Unfortunately, the strike caused the rest of the season to be canceled. That had never happened before. In fact, 1994 turned out to be the first year since 1904 that the World Series wasn't played.

LIFE BEYOND BASEBALL

Luckily for Juan Gonzalez, there is something else in his life besides baseball. It is his devotion to his native country and especially to its young citizens. Helping the people of Puerto Rico has become almost a second full-time job for Juan. He has always returned home as soon as the season ended to work with kids.

One of the things he does is visit elementary schools all around the island. The kids have come to know him on sight, shouting, "Igor, Igor, Igor" as soon as they see him arrive. He mingles with the crowd, signs autographs, and speaks to them. He has a very definite message.

"We live a very complicated life, full of challenges," he tells them. "The best way to approach the life you're living is with education and sports. After God, education and sports are the best tools to defeat any obstacles in your way. One day you may be in a position like me to influence other young ones growing up."

Returning to Puerto Rico in 1994, Juan is mobbed by kids as usual. Notice the sign in the background welcoming "Igor" back. Juan has quickly become a hero in his native land.

His friend Luis Mayoral says he has watched Juan mature over the years. He agrees that Juan is unlike many other stars. "Juan is not in love with money. He has a great social conscience. I haven't seen anyone like him since [Roberto] Clemente. His love for children is genuine. Clemente had that."

The reaction at every school is the same: The kids swarm around Juan, their eyes wide open and big smiles on their faces. During the off-season he visits more than fifty schools, and he loves the attention.

"It's incredible," Juan has said. "But it's incredible every time all over Puerto Rico. Every time."

Another thing Juan has done regularly is visit the Alto de Cuba section where he grew up. He has paid utility bills and bought medicine for those there who need help. He also has held yearly Christmas parties on the streets of the barrio. When he's home, he works out at

Juan's love of children (and their devotion to him) is obvious in this photo.

Juan has signed hundreds of baseballs for his fans.

a tiny gym in the neighborhood, buying vitamins for the boys who lift weights with him.

Although Juan has never been one to talk much about his baseball career, he will speak freely about the injustices he sees in Alto de Cuba and other areas like it.

"It makes me feel bad and sad at the same time," he has said. "The youth is losing its future to drugs. But I also blame the government authorities for not caring for the people of the barrio. There is not a baseball field or a basketball court for them. There is a saying in Spanish that means, 'We criticize but do not help.' That's what happens there."

Juan has also found time to visit prisons and hospitals in Puerto Rico. At the hospitals, Juan has often talked to the children who have been abused or who have had problems with drugs.

"He is simply a person for the people," his friend Luis Mayoral has said.

What lies ahead for Juan in the future is no mystery. He has made no secret of what he will do later in life when he is no longer hitting home runs.

"I will be focused on serving the people of Puerto Rico, not from a political platform, but from a social platform," he has said. "God gave me a good mind and the ability to succeed in baseball. I understand that I have to give back for what God has given me."

As a ballplayer, Juan is still relatively young, but he has the potential to be one of the all-time greats. Devoted to his baseball career, he has purchased a modest house in North Arlington, Texas, only five minutes from the Rangers' new ballpark, which opened in 1994.

"Juan's goals are mostly private," Luis Mayoral has said. "I know he sets a standard of a .300 batting average, 30 homers, and 100 RBI each year. Down the road, however, I think he would like to finish with 400 to 500 home runs. And I know he would like to make the Hall of Fame."

If his first four years in the majors are an indication, Juan Gonzalez is well on his way.

JUAN GONZALEZ: HIGHLIGHTS

1969   Born on October 16 in Vega Baja, Puerto Rico.

1986   Signs with Texas Rangers. Begins professional
        baseball career at Sarasota, Florida, in Gulf Coast League.

1987   Plays with Gastonia in South Atlantic League.

1988   Plays with Charlotte in Florida State League.

1989   Plays with Tulsa in Texas League. Hits 21 home runs
        and bats .293.
        Spends month of September in majors with Texas
        Rangers. Hits first major league home run.

1990   Plays with Oklahoma City in American Association, a
        Class AAA league (highest minor league). Leads
        league with 29 home runs and 101 RBI.
        Joins Texas Rangers in August.

1991   Hits 27 home runs and drives in 102 runs in first full
        season with Rangers.

1992   Leads majors with 43 home runs. Drives in 109 runs.

1993   Leads majors with 46 home runs, drives in 118 runs,
        bats .310.

1994   Strike ends baseball season on August 12.
        In shortened season, bats .275 with 19 home runs and
        85 RBI.

FIND OUT MORE

Duden, Jane. *Baseball*. New York: Macmillan, 1991.

Gilbert, Thomas W. *Roberto Clemente*. New York: Chelsea House, 1991.

Gutman, Bill. *Baseball*. North Bellmore, N.Y.: Marshall Cavendish, 1990.

Kaplan, Rick. *The Official Baseball Hall of Fame Book of Super Stars*. New York: Simon and Schuster, 1989.

Monteleone, John. *A Day in the Life of a Major League Baseball Player*. Mahwah, N.J.: Troll, 1992.

Sally, Dick and Tom Dipace. *Home Run Kings*. New York: Simon and Schuster, 1989.

How to write to Juan Gonzalez:
Juan Gonzalez
c/o Texas Rangers
1000 Ballpark Way
Arlington, TX 76011

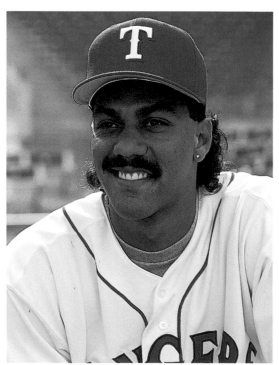

INDEX